MOMO COME HOME

By Bonnie Lee

Bonnie Lee Books
Mountain View, California 94040

ISBN: 978-0-8059-7892-6

Printed in China

Bonnie Lee Books
Mountain View, California 94040

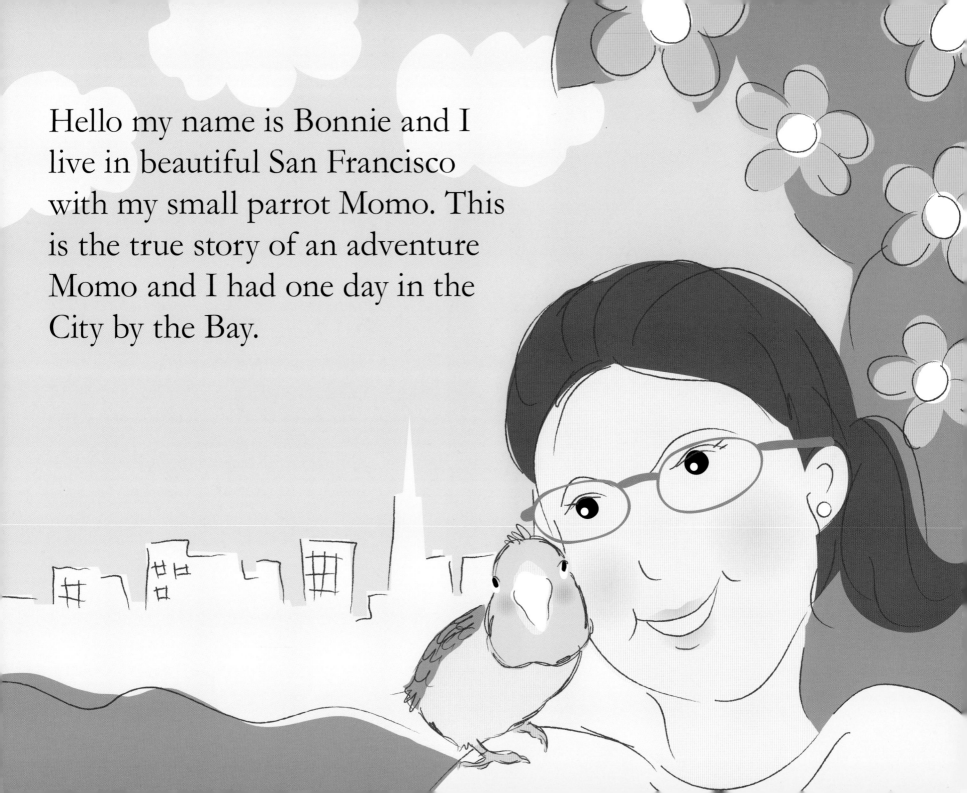

Hello my name is Bonnie and I
live in beautiful San Francisco
with my small parrot Momo. This
is the true story of an adventure
Momo and I had one day in the
City by the Bay.

Saturday morning begins, a day filled with brilliant sunshine and delightfully warm weather in San Francisco. Momo starts to chirp, letting me know that he wants to come out of his cage for his pre-breakfast flight around the apartment.

I tell Momo we are going out for breakfast down on Fillmore Street, a beautiful tree-lined street.

Momo always stays on my shoulder when we go outside. I have no doubt in my mind that today will be the same.

When we arrive at Fillmore Street, I look for a café to have breakfast. Momo enjoys eating bread crumbs and other sweet treats.

Just as I am crossing the street to go to a café, Momo decides to fly away. Oh my, what a big surprise!

MOMO

Momo flies up the street and lands in a tree a block away. I run down to get Momo, but the branch is too high for me to reach him.

I call Momo's name, hoping he will fly down and land back on my shoulder. Unfortunately, Momo has other ideas. Momo stays in the tree and starts climbing to higher branches. I guess he wants to see more of San Francisco.

I don't know what to do, so I decide to call the San Francisco Animal Rescue Center and ask if they can help me get back Momo.

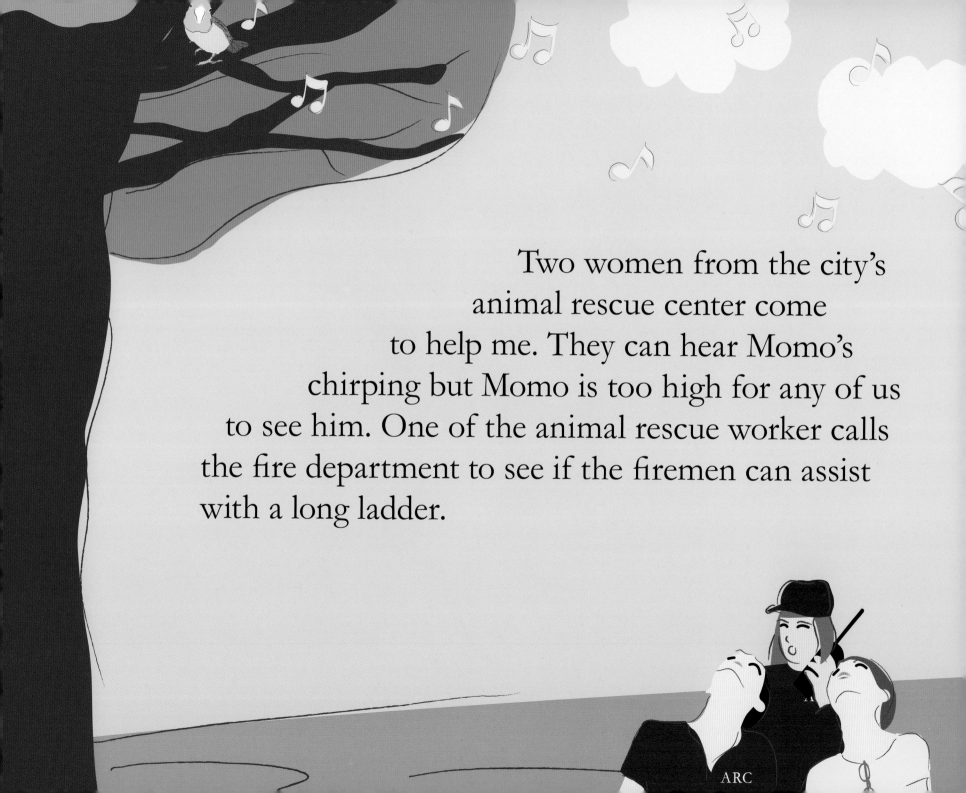

Two women from the city's
animal rescue center come
to help me. They can hear Momo's
chirping but Momo is too high for any of us
to see him. One of the animal rescue worker calls
the fire department to see if the firemen can assist
with a long ladder.

When the firemen arrive, I hope they will be able to rescue Momo.

One fireman carefully places the ladder up against the tree and slowly climbs up the ladder. Just when he is about to save Momo, little Momo flies up to a higher branch!

The fireman says the ladder can't reach Momo up so high. He tells me that Momo is in his natural setting and that there is nothing more the firemen can do.

I can't leave little Momo all alone in the tree. He has never been on his own before.

It is getting very dark outside. All of our rescue efforts have failed. I can't believe that I may never see or hear my Momo again.

After hours trying to see Momo up in the tree and listening for his chirp, I sadly decide to go back to my parents' home.

When I arrive, my dad suggests that we make reward posters and put them where we last saw Momo. We hope that someone will find him and call the phone number on the poster, so we can rescue Momo.

My dad and I go back to Fillmore Street so we can tape the posters to street light poles.

My dad and I walk up and down the street calling Momo's name. We listen carefully for Momo's chirp, but we don't hear a sound.

Then in the distance
we hear a faint
chirp. Could it be
Momo's chirp?

It is Momo's chirp! But where is Momo? The sound is not coming from the tree where we last saw him? Where can Momo be?

We run up the street calling "Momo! Momo! Where are you?" This time we hear his chirp, and it is a lot stronger! We keep calling out his name. "Momo! Momo!" We look all around in the direction of the chirps, which are getting louder.

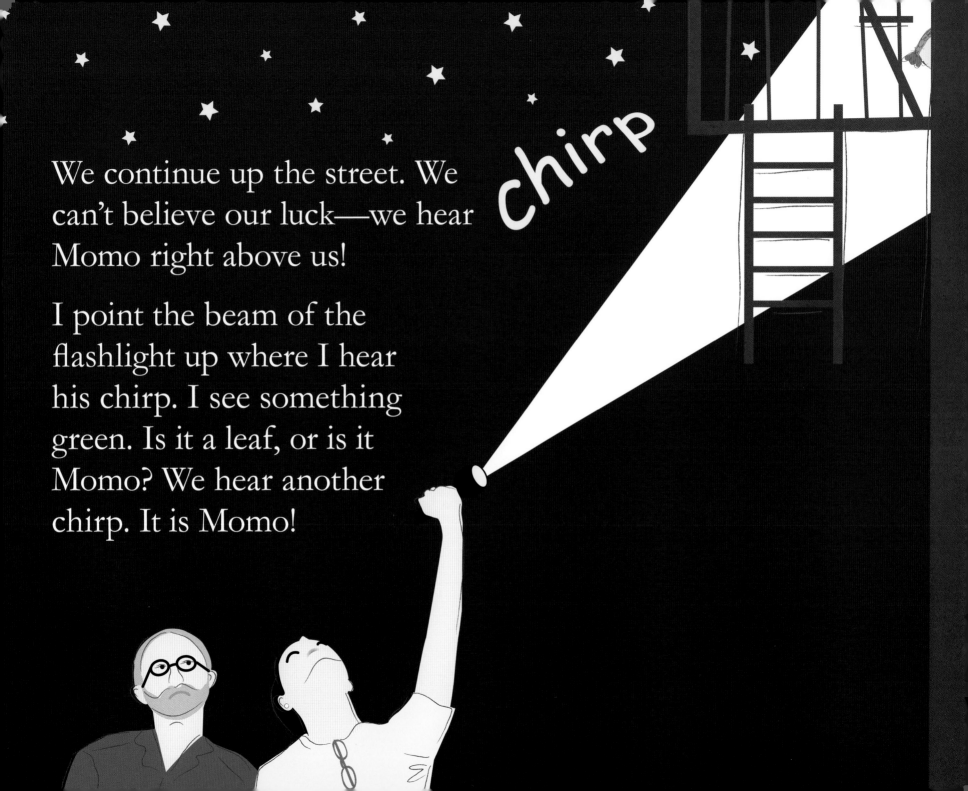

We continue up the street. We can't believe our luck—we hear Momo right above us!

I point the beam of the flashlight up where I hear his chirp. I see something green. Is it a leaf, or is it Momo? We hear another chirp. It is Momo!

chirp

Little Momo is on the fire escape too high for us to reach. The building is locked for the night. Oh, little Momo is so close, and yet so far!

Again I
call the
Animal Rescue
Control. I tell
them I found little Momo,
but I can't reach him. They
tell me they will call the fire
department to assist with
rescuing Momo.

When the firemen arrive and see where Momo is, they say that their truck doesn't have a ladder long enough to reach Momo. I am so sad.

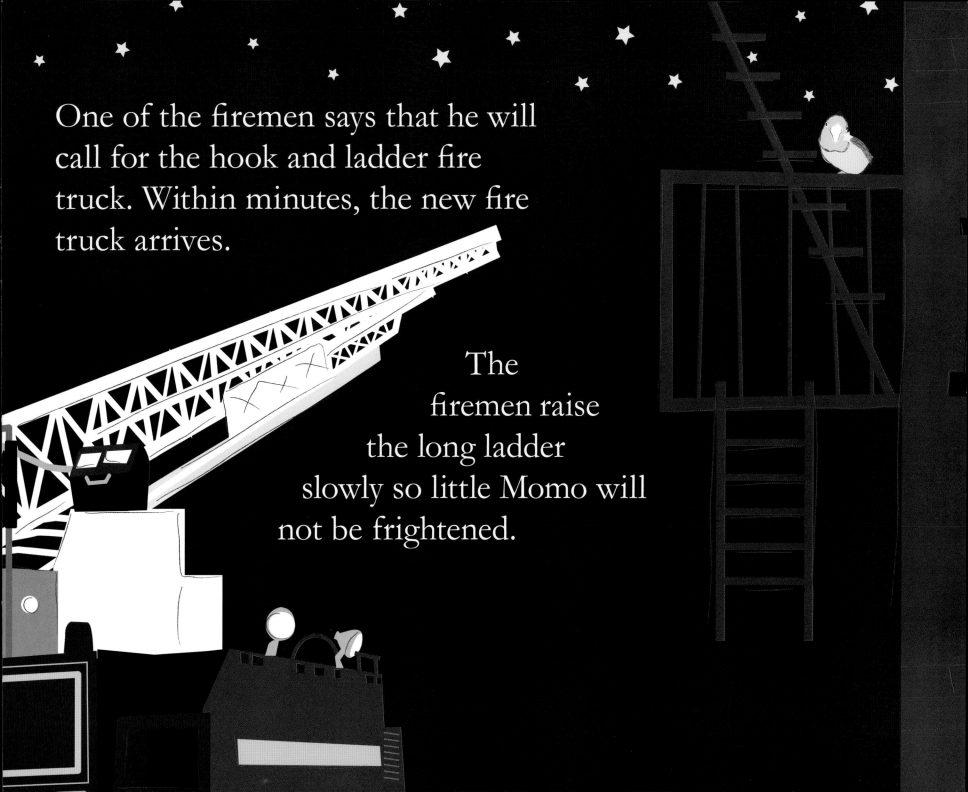

One of the firemen says that he will call for the hook and ladder fire truck. Within minutes, the new fire truck arrives.

The firemen raise the long ladder slowly so little Momo will not be frightened.

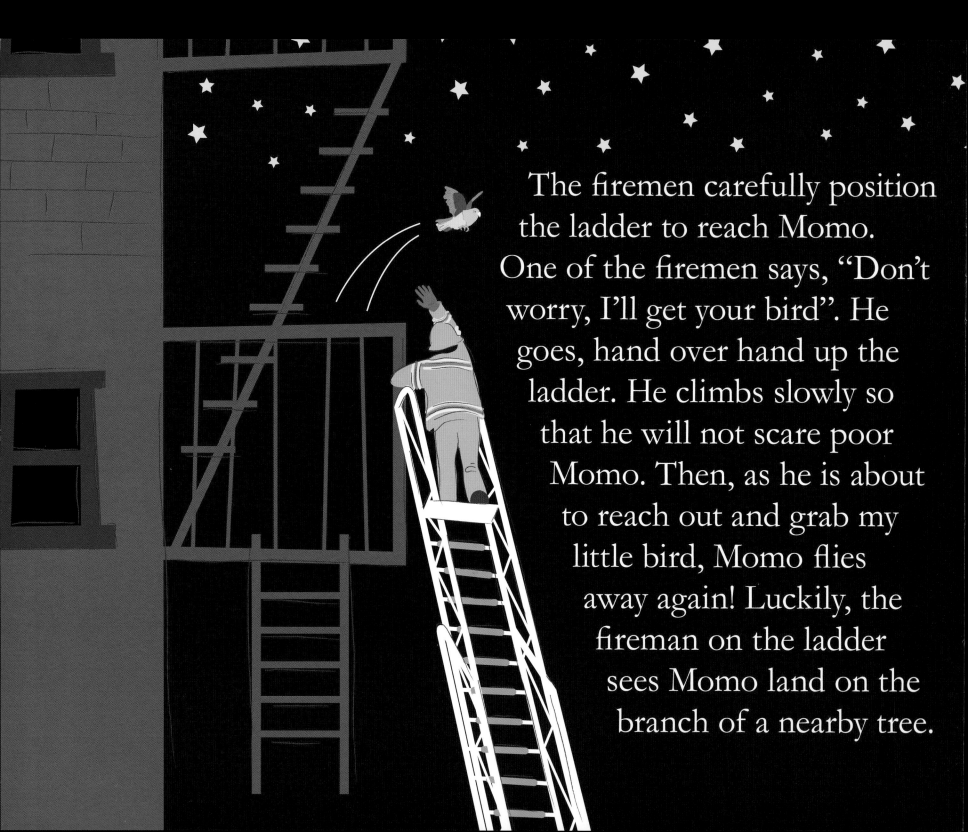

The firemen carefully position the ladder to reach Momo. One of the firemen says, "Don't worry, I'll get your bird". He goes, hand over hand up the ladder. He climbs slowly so that he will not scare poor Momo. Then, as he is about to reach out and grab my little bird, Momo flies away again! Luckily, the fireman on the ladder sees Momo land on the branch of a nearby tree.

The firemen are called to an emergency and have to leave. They wish us good luck with little Momo. The fire engine pulls away and in the silence of the evening I hear Momo chirping. We have tried everything to rescue him.

chirp chirp chirp chirp chirp

Just then, my dad sees a shooting star fly across the night sky and tells me to make a wish. All I want is for Momo to come back to me; that is my wish.

Dad has a plan, he tells
me he will climb up the
tree. Up and up he goes.
Dad shakes the branches
and Momo flies to a
lower branch.

Momo sees
me under
the tree
and hangs upside
down smiling at me.

My dad gives the branch
a final mighty shake.
Momo drops down a
bit, then starts to get
ready for another flight
into the evening air. But
before he can fly, I jump
up and catch him. I
catch Momo in midair!

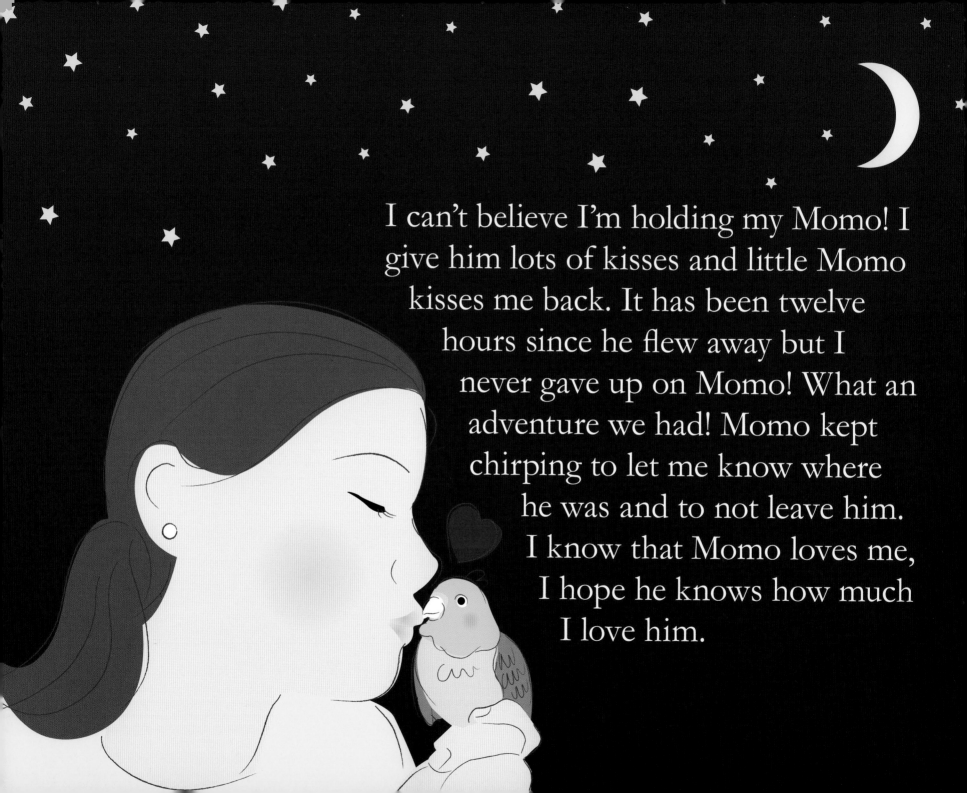

I can't believe I'm holding my Momo! I give him lots of kisses and little Momo kisses me back. It has been twelve hours since he flew away but I never gave up on Momo! What an adventure we had! Momo kept chirping to let me know where he was and to not leave him. I know that Momo loves me, I hope he knows how much I love him.

Turn the page to color your very own Momo!

Want to color more?

Please visit Bonnie Lee Books at www.bonnieleebooks.com

Click on the coloring tab to download a coloring page from the collection of Bonnie Lee Books.

Have Fun!